After finishing her law degree, Stacey Dixon Phelan knew her most important contribution would be raising her two daughters and son. As a stay-at-home mother, she found tremendous inspiration for writing.

More Than All the Pastries in Paris began as a game with her children as she would say goodnight, explaining, "I love you more than the moon and stars." To this, they surprised her with responses that would be impossible to count, exhibiting a level of imagination that only children could possess.

This is Stacey's first book. She lives in Connecticut with her husband and three children.

More Than All the Pastries in Paris

STACEY DIXON PHELAN

Austin Macauley Publishers™

London • Cambridge • New York • Sharjah

TA CIP catalogue record for this title is available from the British Library.

ISBN 9781398433977 (Paperback)
ISBN 9781398433984 (Hardback)
ISBN 9781786298324 (ePub e-book)

www.austinmacauley.com

First Published (2021)
Austin Macauley Publishers Ltd
25 Canada Square
Canary Wharf
London
E14 5LQ

To Lexi, Sam and Jack – I love you more than the moon
and stars!

I would like to thank the team at Austin Macauley for making this book possible. I am forever grateful to my parents for instilling within me the love of travel and the motivation to recreate the same magic of experiencing the world with my own children. And to my husband, Matty, thank you for chasing this dream with me!

"How much do you love me, Mama?"
asks my sweet child.

"I love you more than all the pastries in Paris."

“More than all the ruins in Rome?”

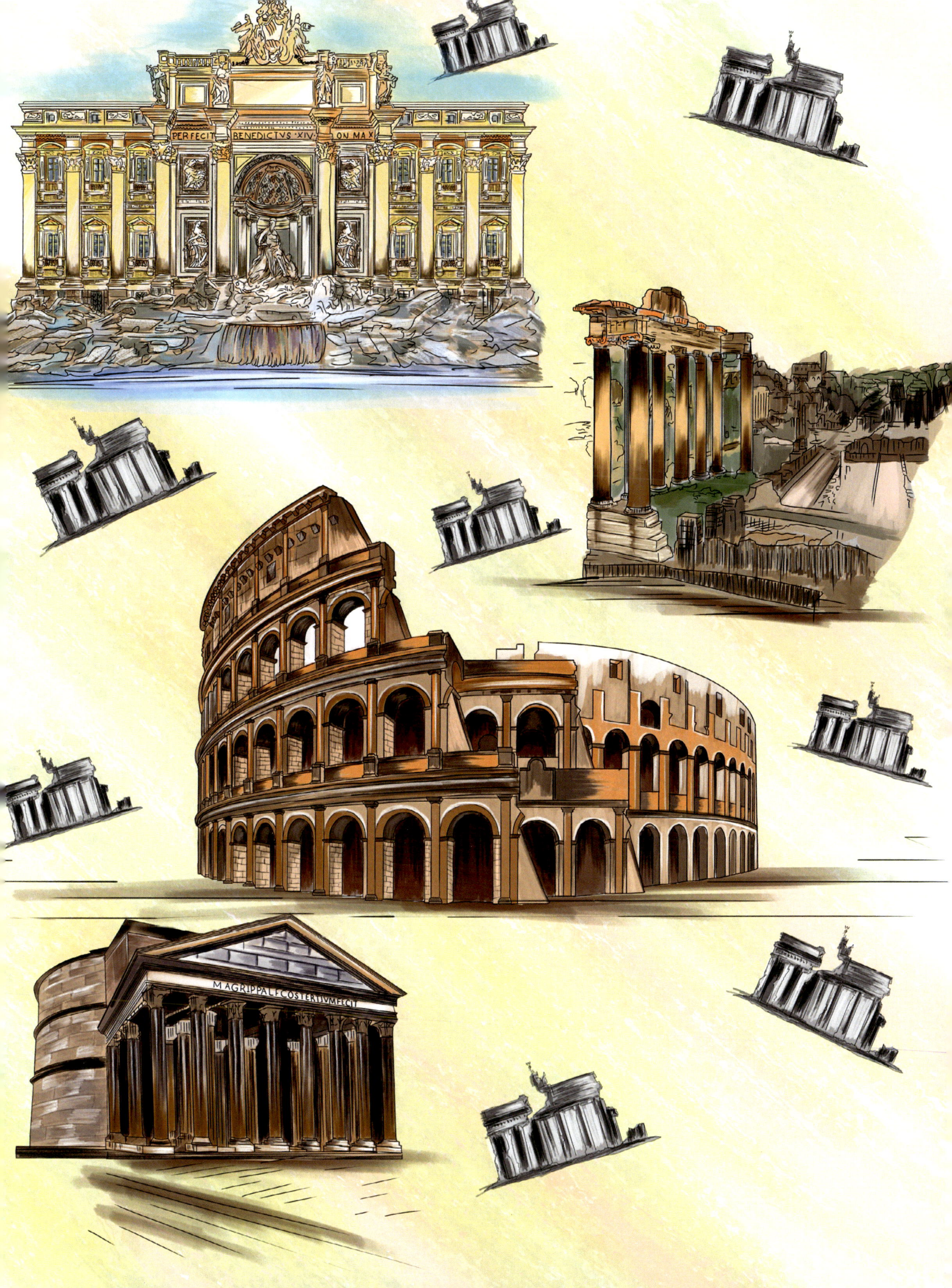
PERFECIT BENEDICTVS ·XIV· ON MAX
M AGRIPPA L F COS TERTIVM FECIT

"More than all the literature in London!"

Shelley
Shakespeare
Austen
Dickens
Brontë
Keats
Dahl
THE WORLD OF JACK LONDON
BOOKS

"How much Mama,
how much do you love me?"

asks my curious child again.

"I love you more than all the maracas
in Madrid."

“More than all the clovers in Killarney?”

"More than all the apple strudel in Amsterdam!"

"Tell me, Mama, tell me how much you love me,"
said my sleepy child.

"I love you more than all the music in Munich."

"More than all the puppets in Prague?"

"More than all the violins in Vienna!"

"Again,"

whispers my child.

"I love you more than all the snowflakes in St. Petersburg!"

Now finally asleep,

my beautiful child.

"One more."

I whisper back.

"I love you more than all the sunsets
in Santorini!"

PLAY THE GAME!
I love you more than.....